I0467191

GREG B RYCZKOWSKI

7 Ways to Make Money in Real Estate

Copyright © 2024 by Greg B Ryczkowski

All rights reserved. No part of this publication may be reproduced, stored or transmitted in any form or by any means, electronic, mechanical, photocopying, recording, scanning, or otherwise without written permission from the publisher. It is illegal to copy this book, post it to a website, or distribute it by any other means without permission.

Greg B Ryczkowski asserts the moral right to be identified as the author of this work.

Greg B Ryczkowski has no responsibility for the persistence or accuracy of URLs for external or third-party Internet Websites referred to in this publication and does not guarantee that any content on such Websites is, or will remain, accurate or appropriate.

Designations used by companies to distinguish their products are often claimed as trademarks. All brand names and product names used in this book and on its cover are trade names, service marks, trademarks and registered trademarks of their respective owners. The publishers and the book are not associated with any product or vendor mentioned in this book. None of the companies referenced within the book have endorsed the book.

First edition

This book was professionally typeset on Reedsy.
Find out more at reedsy.com

Contents

1

Introduction

Hi, I am Greg and I came from Poland, a place where doing business was close to impossible due to the political structure of the country at the time. After learning that real estate is the best method to get ahead, and to hedge against inflation I focused on my personal edification and development skills. According to, https://due.com/unmasking-the-real-estate-wealth-myth , 90 % of big fortune is created in real estate investments and only the remaining 10% is made in big business.

Those who made money in big business have invested their money in real estate anyhow. On that note, we decided to pursue a real estate development avenue. Since we did not know English, had no money, no marketable skills, nor did we have any real business experience it was a tough and slow start. Our first objective was to learn basic English for day to day communication, next was to acquire business vocabulary specific to different sectors. Fortunately, the local Community Colleges system offered English as a second language, business law, preparing business plans, classes about asset protection, finances, accounting, tax return preparation, among, and a myriad of other valuable courses. Also, I found a job in a tile setting company, then I moved up to learning stone fabrication, and also other construction skills. Those jobs not only moved me closer towards my goal but also helped me to put food on the table. Alongside, we have learned another valuable skill, saving money.

During that period I got my hands on various financial courses, one of them was a tax return program. Every bit of my free time I would spend learning the IRS tax code. Passing the final test gave me enough confidence to start preparing taxes for myself and others.

At some point, I was presented with an opportunity to open my own stone fabrication and installation company and I took it. My new workplaces consisted of working in affluent places, wineries in Napa, expensive houses in Tiburon, San Francisco, Hillsborough, Atherton, Los Alto Hills, parts of Saratoga, Cupertino, and Los Gatos. I was able to meet and interact with very successful people like Berry Levinson in Ross, a film director, MC Hammer in Fremont, an American rapper, Francis Coppola in San Francisco, an American film director, Blackhawk/Danville developer, and many others who influenced my life in business and personal development. Although I did not have a close relationship with these people, I was able to observe them, ask questions, and get some ideas from their success. All these people were very happy to share information, ideas and even some of their network. I started having access to a bunch of businesspeople, money lenders, good real estate agents and many others that later on became part of my network. In order to run my business properly, I had to start applying my theoretical knowledge in sales and marketing, entity structuring, asset protection, tax ramification, HR, bookkeeping and accounting, cash flow and investment, and many other aspects.

After two years we saved enough money for a downpayment to buy our first home in Hayward. We got very lucky because that house appreciated quickly right after we bought it, so we were able to cash out about $ 50,000 and use that money to invest in a purchase of a house in Palo Alto, in the city where Stanford University is located. That was the year 1991, a great buyers market in the San Francisco Bay Area. Meanwhile I got a Real Estate Salesperson license, Masonry license, Tile license, and finally General Contractor license.

2

What To Expect

You can expect to be confident and well versed in the real estate market dealings. You can expect to have enough information and self assurance to acquire a property with a very little or no risk involved.

First of all, I would suggest reading through this material, mark interesting passages, highlight, underline, doggie ear pages to have pertinent material to stand out. Start mastering real estate business language, and see which of these methods suit you the most to operate with passion and conviction. Then identify the market that you want to work in. Do not be afraid to talk to real estate professionals, they are very accommodating and easy to work with. To be successful with your first purchase, do your homework, know what you want., so you are not convinced by a listing agent to step into a deal that would not suit your criteria. Read this book again and again to understand in depth the seven techniques. Use this book as a guide when you go on the hunt to buy your first house. Carry a hard copy with you, or have a soft copy on your phone, it will bring you success. You will find answers for your concerns inside this book.

Remember, it is ok to make mistakes, it is ok to make a blunder, it is ok to negotiate, it is ok to ask "stupid" questions. This is a learning curve that will propel you to success. Just remember one thing, when you get into any deal make sure you have contingencies stipulated into the contract, so you always have a way out. The easiest indication of the value of your deal is how this property attracts private money i.e. hard money lenders. If the deal is good they will throw money at you insisting on closing the deal with them. They will compete between other hard money lenders for your business. If the deal is so so, or bad you will be asked to bring a large down payment. Run away from that deal then. After learning and applying techniques from this book, you may regard yourself as a real estate expert. Each of these methods has been successfully implemented in real life. All these seven ways have brought revenue and profits. They produced wealth!!!

3

Prepare yourself; learn the Real Estate language

G et familiar with Real Estate terminology. Start going to the open houses and talk to the Real Estate Agents, they have their own language/jargon that you need to be familiar with. It is all right to be a laity at first. Please ask questions when something throws you off, listing agents, loan agents, will be pleased to explain the meanings and procedures. On the top of these, start building your own database of professionals to expand your access to the market. Create a database of listing agents, banks, private money lenders, (You can see the example of such in your resources section) Title Companies and their officers, potential sellers and buyers. Find professionals flipping houses, buy them lunch and listen to their stories and techniques they use. This is a fun business if you approach it right. Take it slowly and without huge expectations. At the beginning it will be slow and might be painful. This is your University, but your diploma will be invaluable.

Do not omit learning from each and every person that is doing a business and is a leader. Even if they fail, look at what they have done wrong and do the opposite. The smartest way to learn is to capitalize

on someone else's mistakes. Good luck !!!.

4

The Seven Methods

The 20/80 method.
The second method 10/80/10.
The 65/35 technique.
Another 65/35 method with a twist.
Lease with an option to buy.
Shared Equity Partnership.
Cash out at the Close of Escrow.

Start from finding the right location for you. I suggest you stay close to where you live, your workplace, and your family. It is crucial, especially for investment properties to be within your quick reach, so you can immediately address any issues that will arise. Drive through those neighborhoods mornings, afternoons, and at night. Observe who lives there, the lifestyle, is this neighborhood safe, how is traffic at various hours. Search demographics, schools, median income, find out if most of these houses are rented, or owned, look up the crime rate, etc. Try to connect with someone that is already doing what you want to do.When you are stepping into a deal, first order of business is what is my exit strategy?

The 20/80 method.

The first method to buy your home is by using 20% of your own money and 80% of Institutional/ Banks money. You need to make sure you have an extra 1-3% for the closing costs. Ask the agent to give you an estimated closing cost calculation. Get pre-approved for the loan, before making offers. This is one of the documents needed along with your offer to strengthen your position. Ask the listing agent to represent you, this is called a "dual agency". Some agents would refuse to engage in doing that, but more often than not they will find a way to retain a full commission. I used this strategy with my very first flip. A friend of mine, a General Contractor and I combined our forces and bought a fixer upper in Menlo Park on Laurel Ave. Within a year we made about $ 200,000 of a net profit. For this purpose we created a C Corporation to protect our personal assets and separate accounting from the personal one. At the end of the year, we had to pay short term capital gain taxes because the deal was executed within a year.

The second method is the 10/80/10 method.

It goes like this: you save 10 % of the purchase price, have a bank to finance 80% and the last 10% find from other resources. It means borrowing from your friends, family members, private small investors, etc. That 10% of the purchase price will be recorded as a 2nd position lien. You can consolidate the loans on that property as quickly as in four to six months and pay off the 2nd position lien holder. In today's world, it is much easier to refinance an asset that you are in possession of, than obtaining financing for a new purchase. Remember to be ready with an extra 1-3% for closing costs. This method was used by me on a flip in Palo Alto on Emerson St. We have used the same Corporation as in Menlo Park. The Emerson project lasted longer than one year therefore our capital gain taxes were long term therefore by 5 percent lower.

The 65/35 technique.

The third approach, especially in the sellers' market, is this 65/35 method. You borrow 65% of hard money for a first position lien and put down 35% of your own money. It's a quick close of escrow approach, within a two weeks time frame. Afterwards, you can do a light remodeling and refinance it. Banks will refinance that property in a four to six month period. The 35 % amount does not have to be your own money, it could be OPM – Other People's Money. Reach out to small investors. Oftentimes, they are not able to buy real estate because they don't know how to use these techniques, nor do they have enough money to buy a house outright. We have used that particular play flipping a property in Palo Alto on Palo Alto Ave. Initially, our C Corporation was on the title, then we switched that to our personal name since we moved in for two years taking advantage of capital gain tax write off law.

Another 65/35 method with a seller's carry.

Another 65/35 acquisition technique goes as follows. You ask the seller to carry a loan of 35% in the second position. The seller's money is secured by the house and there are no capital gain taxes for the seller until they get their principle from your pay off. Make sure you have an extra 1-3% of the total purchase price as reserves to close escrow. Always, always ask the listing agent to represent you. Oftentimes I would ask the seller to carry even more than 35%. The interest rate on such a loan is usually much lower than the hard money one. Ask the Title Company Officer to help you with preparation of all needed documentation. We used this particular strategy to flip a house on Madison Ave in San Jose. Owner carried 35%, the hard money lender carried 65%, so we just paid for closing costs. This seller needed a three year lease back and paid us rents. For three years the seller lived in the house, took care of it as well as for the whole property. We held this property inside of a self directed ROTH IRA account, so no capital gain taxes upon the sale.

Lease with an option to buy.

Lease with an option to buy is yet another method of getting a property. Usual terms for that type of deal are as follows: 5 years lease with a possibility of an extension for another five year segment. You can exercise the option at any time during the five-year lease period. Normally, the property owner would require at least 3% of the security deposit, that money goes towards the purchase if you exercise the option, or stays with the seller if you do not. Also, the monthly rent payments consist of regular payment plus extra money that is returned to you at the time of purchase. Your security deposit might be met with some other valuables like a car, jewelry, paintings, collectibles, etc. The great thing about this is that you are locking up the purchase price.

Shared Equity Partnership.

Shared Equity Partnering is the sixth method of acquisition. Similarly to lease with an option to buy, the shared equity technique allows some buyers that are not quite ready yet to get into a property, tie up some of the loose ends in their personal lives and close escrow in two or three years while enjoying the house while making money on the increased equity. Again, you need a security deposit and higher monthly rent to get into a contract similar to the lease with the option to buy technique. In this case you agree to a certain price in the future however, the appreciated value gets split 50/50 after you deduct any incurred expenses for remodeling, addition, or major repairs. Find a customer who has got some money, but is not ready to buy the property right that moment. They might need to improve their credit score, or their family affairs are just not quite cleared up, or something of that nature. Your advantage is that the potential buyer is taking care of the property and makes sure not to skip any payments, not to lose their investment. People have all sorts of different challenges, this might be just a suitable scenario for them.

Cash out at the Close of Escrow.

The seventh method is a combination of hard money, and sellers carry, except the combined amount constitutes more than 100 % of the purchase price. You cash out the excess at the close of escrow. This operation it's plausible in the buyer's market and requires lots of repairs, or the seller needs cash quickly. These circumstances have to be just right to play that scenario. We used this technique in a sellers market for a three-plex on Middlefield in Palo Alto.

5

Seven Methods of Financing the Purchase

Your own savings, retirement accounts, inheritance.
Institutional large Bank.
Small Credit Union Banks.
Family and Friends.
Hard money lenders.
Money partnerships.
Creating your own Fund.

Your own savings, retirement accounts, inheritance.

The easiest investment is when you have money ready to be deployed. That could be your savings account, your 401K, your IRA, your inheritance, big bonus, proceeds from a sale of a business etc. This is a very rare situation, so you most likely need to employ other methods. However, saving money is a very good habit. Make it automatic, send it directly from your paycheck or other income resource to your money management account. It will accumulate while you slip and you adjust your expenses to your income accordingly.

Here is a tip for your money management:
Use the 70/10/10/10 method. Give 10% of your net income away, 10% goes to pay down your debt, 10% goes to your savings account, and you live on the remaining 70% of your income.

Institutional large Bank.

Institutional banks are the second way of financing your deal. They require tons of paperwork. They are slow these days and difficult to work with. In the sellers market you might find them to be impractical since they are unreliable, and they take "forever". Because of that you might lose the deal. In time like that sellers have others ready to buy and their money is available without any contingencies.

Small Credit Union Banks.

Credit Unions are small family types of banks that allow you to have a personal relationship with the owners and personnel. Even though their paperwork might be demanding also, the loan officer would gladly help you with each step of the way. Build up a relationship by opening an account there, borrowing money from them to finance a car to establish a trusting relationship. Make deposits in person and get to know the manager and personnel. Usually, there are five to eight people working at a branch. Open CD's (Certificates of Deposit) and keep on utilizing their services, so they will be glad to jump in and help with your home loan when you are ready to buy. Prepare the ground.

Family and Friends.

Some of us have wealthy family and friends that want to invest their money in a private adventure such as flipping houses. They would invest with you because of your character and integrity. When asking for investment, be ready to show them all the numbers and explain how you will make money for them. They are already willing to work with you, build their trust by being professional and knowledgeable. Most people are dreaming of investment and flipping houses. They have heard of many successful investors like Kyosaki or Trump, maybe someone locally. This might be their way to start the life adventure with you, spearheading the action.

Hard money lenders.

There are private money lenders that are looking for deals to employ their money. These people do not want a hustle of becoming a partner, but want a share of the "pie" in the form of interest and points. We call this source smart money. Hard money lenders would not invest in a bad deal, hence they will help you to select the right deal. If the private money does not want to invest, run from the deal, most likely it is not good for you. Lenders of hard money are the best teachers and will give you expertise free of charge. Do not be swayed by any listing agent or a homeowner to buy a property unless they are willing to invest with you on such a deal. FYI, listing agents' role is to sell the property, not to give you sound advice on investing.

Bringing on a money partner.

You may start from setting up a database of potential money partners. There are three ways of rewarding your potential investors; one is equity partnership, second one is giving them interest on their money, the third one is a combination of the two. The most efficient way to invest is to deal with only one person, because you come to consensus much faster then with a group. Efficiency is always the key. Even if you have a number of investors, try to designate only one to deal with if at all possible. In case of a deal going "south" make sure you take care of the investors first. They will greatly appreciate it and most likely come back to support you in the future.

Creating your own LLC Fund.

Another way of financing the deal is to create a Fund that collects money from a number of investors. You can put together a mix of small and larger chunks. My minimum investment from a single person was $ 50,000. Make sure you have appropriate disclosures. For guidance connect with a lawyer and an accountant, specialists who have done it already. As usual, all these dealings are up for negotiation, but remember to be fair. Make sure you will update your investors regularly. If the fund is just sitting at the bank in money order or CD mode, I would suggest doing updates once a month. If the fund is activated and deployed, the frequency of the updates should be once a week. Do not hold back neither good, nor bad news. Your team might have solutions for the challenges at hand. Leverage their money, resources, networks, and mental capacity. Learn how other investors are handling these types of partnerships. They will appreciate your attitude and ethics.

6

Tax Advantages and Asset Protection.

Self Directed IRA.
Business Trust.
Non-Grantor, Irrevocable, Complex, Discretionary, Spendthrift Trust.
Land title.
Limited Liability Company.
TIC.
Mix methods.

Self Directed IRA.

O pen your retirement account with a self directed IRA Custodian. I personally use Forge Trust, and KKOS lawyers, mat@kkoslawyers.com If you are moving money from a traditional Custodian, what usually you need to do is to cash out your positions inside your account and move cash. Do not remove cash from your account, make sure you transfer it directly from one retirement account Custodian to another. Otherwise you might incur capital gain taxes. The best retirement account to use for your deals, as far as tax savings go, is to use your ROTH IRA. When you receive money from your investments inside the ROTH IRA account all income is tax free. When you invest in other ira accounts all income is tax deferred. Consult your tax professional to double check this avenue as the tax code is changing constantly.

Disclaimer:

I am not a licensed tax or legal advisor. I do not give tax, legal, or accounting advice. This material has been prepared for informational purposes only, and is not intended to provide, and should not be relied upon for tax, legal, or accounting purposes. Please, consult a professional for tax, legal, or accounting advice before applying these into works and transactions.

Business Trust.

After congress implemented the Corporate Transparency Act in 2022, almost all small business owners have to get FinCen number. With this bill the assumption of our Congress is that we are all criminals and need to prove to the governing authority otherwise. Our business operation will be inspected constantly by an Artificial Intelligence program 24/7. On top of it, banks are compelled to report irregularities in our banking patterns. It is a total invigilation, but for now we need to comply with that. At this point Corporations and LLC's are obsolete, they are failing us. To avoid all of this mess, we need to resort to an entity called Business Trust. This legal structure is not obligated to get the FinCen number, we circumvent state reporting and it allows more tax deductible items. Run your business in a Business Trust that gives you 100 % asset protection and significantly reduces your taxes, better than you can do with an LLC or an S Corporation.

The Business Trust has the following stipulations. It can receive active business Income, and it is a pass through entity.

Business Trust operates as a regular business, it performs the same functions. You open a business account with a bank, invoice the customers, etc. Revenue comes in, you deduct all operating expenses and allowable costs and the net profit goes to Non-Grantor, Irrevocable, Complex, Discretionary Spendthrift Trust. Tax return zeros out. Some states may not want to issue a license to a Business Trust, but you need to inquire about this in your state and licensing board.

Disclaimer:

I am not a licensed tax or legal advisor. I do not give tax, legal, or accounting advice. This material has been prepared for informational purposes only, and is not intended to provide, and should not be relied upon for tax, legal, or accounting purposes. Please, consult a professional for tax, legal, or accounting advice before applying these into works and transactions.

You may find all info on Youtube by Don Thornton and other professionals.

Non-Grantor, Irrevocable, Complex, Discretionary, Spendthrift Trust.

The full name of this vehicle is a mouthful, Non-Grantor, Irrevocable, Complex Discretionary, Spendthrift Trust, where you are a trustee and do not own anything, but you decide on all the assets inside that trust. You are tax exempt from the following income: interest, royalties, limited partnership income, lease income, and rental income. With this Trust one can run an unlimited number of projects to create a few income streams, open an unlimited number of bank accounts and report everything on one tax return (Form 1041). All Passive income is non-taxable, capital gains taxes eliminated, 100% lawsuit-Proof Asset Protection, and IRS Code 643 (b) compliant. It is important to remember that this trust can only receive passive income. As a trustee, you can declare as an extraordinary dividend all money coming in, and by doing so it is not considered income.

IRS Code 643(b): Extraordinary Dividend (b) income. "For purposes of this subpart and and subpart B, C, and D the term "income" when not proceed by by the words "taxable", "distributable net", "undistributed net", or "gross", means the amount of income of the estate or trust for the taxable year determined under the terms of the governing instrument and applicable local law. Items of gross income constituting extraordinary dividends or taxable stock dividends which the fiduciary (trustee), acting in good faith, determines to be allocable to corpus (to the Trust) under the terms of the governing instrument and applicable local law shall not be considered income". Furthermore the code stipulates on Capital Gains Tax Exclusions in point (3) Capital Gains and Losses:

"Gains from the sale or exchange of capital assets shall be excluded to the extent that such gains are allocated to corpus (meaning Trust) and are not (A) paid, permanently set aside, or to be used for the purpose specified in section 642 c". For the exclusion to be valid the IRS requires compliance with 646 (b). It has to be a correct Trust; Non-Grantor, Irrevocable, Complex, Discretionary. The funds have to be allocated to the corpus, and can not be required to distribute to the beneficiaries.

The Beneficial Trust has the following:

· Spendthrift Provision.
· Can Only Receive Passive Income.
· Holds Personal and Business Assets.
· Recipient of Funds from Business Trust.

Disclaimer:

I am not a licensed tax or legal advisor. I do not give tax, legal, or accounting advice. This material has been prepared for informational purposes only, and is not intended to provide, and should not be relied upon for tax, legal, or accounting purposes. Please, consult a professional for tax, legal, or accounting advice before applying these into works and transactions.

Land Trust.

Land Trust will also work as an entity to buy and sell real estate. Legally recognizable vehicle, Title holding Trust, a contract, it's completely private. A contract stipulating how much control you give to the Trustee, how much you give to the beneficiary or beneficiaries. A great asset and liability protection play because you are removing your name from the title, hence one can not sue you to get to the property. It works like Revocable Living Trust. You need three parties to it, Grantor, Trustee and Beneficiary. The Trustee does not have to be an individual, you can use for example a Wyoming LLC. On the top of it, this could be the same individual for all three, but not recommended. It is a great tool, especially for beginning investors. One piece of paper transfers to anyone or any entity to assign the title and it's not recorded anywhere. Flipping the property to investors from the land Trust gives you additional benefits. Ease of moving property between entities and individuals is enormous. Remember to make yourself a Trustee, then you can freerely manage the financial side of the business. Make sure your beneficiary is an entity that can handle capital gain taxes. It might be a retirement account. That does not mean that an individual is prohibited to take that place. You should use a beneficiary that would reinvest the funds in the future projects. This play is all up to you.

Limited Liability Company.

The old way, before The Corporate Transparency Act implementation of the best entities to deal flips in was an LLC. It is still a valid vehicle. It does not give you as much asset protection as it used to, and you need to get a FinCen number for it and do additional reporting. However, this type of entity will give you additional tax write offs and more protection than going on the title as an individual. LLC would allow you to pull in a few partners and sign an LLC side Agreement to operate. You stay as member/manager of such LLC and your investment partners money is secured by that agreement, but they do not have managerial capacity.

TIC.

TIC stands for Tenants In Common property title vesting. This works with a number of individuals going directly on the title. Those people can come in as individuals or companies with percentage share stipulated on the title. This type of setting is a little more cumbersome as everyone can be a manager and make decisions. With Tenants in Common vesting everyone's investment is fully protected by the deed of trust. This way is much easier to convince investors to join you on that deal. Also, all proceeds are sorted out in the escrow. You do not need to run additional accounting figures, nor do you need to do additional tax reporting. Furthermore, all investors agree on the split right there and then and basically forfeit any recourse afterwards. This is a great way to indemnify yourself from a potential future liability. Combination of those.

Keep it in the right entity – more tax advantages and asset protection. Increase value with sweat equity.

7

Action Steps and Conclusion

R ead the book a number of times to perfect these given strategies.

Create a database of Real Estate professionals, hard money lenders, bank representatives, loan officers, Title Companies officers, potential investors, Contractors, Suppliers

How to work your database daily. Create a spreadsheet as your database of your network. On the top across insert the following labels, name, phone number, email address, date for contact number one, date for contact number two, date for contact number three, and last column with comments. Make sections of Real Estate professionals, Hard Money Lenders, Bank Representatives, Loan Officers, Title companies and officers, Potential Investors, Contractors, Suppliers, Potential Property Sellers, Potential Property Buyers. In each section place three new names every day and contact three potential clients every day. Start with your circle of influence i.e. your phone contacts. When you exhaust your contacts, start asking those people from your database for referrals, leverage their contacts. Be consistent, like a clockwork make sure you designate one hour quiet time, no interruption to work on your database.

Find a suitable house, think of a couple of acquisition strategies, approach the listing agent and ask them to represent you. Be prepared with POF, proof of funds, LOI, letter of intent, In some cases you will start with LOI. Check your FICO score, you will need it to be approved for a loan by the bank, a seller, or even a business partner or an investor. When you are prepared, you will present yourself trustworthy to your partners. You will make more money as a result. At the beginning this whole business might be a little scary, but everything you want is just outside of your comfort zone.

If you do not have a good steady job start a construction, lending, real estate salesperson business. Those could be complimentary opening the door to further access to the market.

About This Book

If you are planning to make money in real estate, then this book will lead you by hand through a few possible scenarios of real life opportunities. By knowing these details, you will avoid serious mistakes that will not only save you money, but will put cash in your pocket. This book will answer many of your concerns and will show you where to start your journey.

What is included here:

- Seven different real life scenarios of how to acquire a property.
- Seven ways of financing such deals.
- Practical ways of preparing yourself for this profession.
- How to recognize a good deal.
- Some exit strategies to make money.

This practical guide will meet you wherever you are at present and quickly swing you into action with confidence and assurance towards your goal. Examples used in this book are actual deals made by the author.

If you are ready to make serious money for generations to come, look no further, scroll up and click the buy button. Enjoy the content and build wealth!

www.ingramcontent.com/pod-product-compliance
Lightning Source LLC
Chambersburg PA
CBHW070442240526
45479CB00012B/339